If I Can Help Somebody

If I Can Help Somebody...

First Paperback edition June 2020
ISBN: 978-0-578-68418-5

Cover and Book Design: Dania Zafar
Copy Editor: Ryan Archer

If I Can Help Somebody...

Ceola Brown Loan

CONTENTS

Introduction

If I Can Help Somebody is a song written by Alma Bazel Androzzo Thompson, in 1945. I first heard it in church when I was a young girl; its message touched my heart and remained with me for the rest of my life. The message that we are called to help each other - whether through a smile, an encouraging word or an outstretched hand - is the theme that runs through the stories in this book.

These stories are a compilation of wonderful encounters - some fleeting and others occurring over a period of time. Some were chance meetings with strangers who became co-travelers on my life's journey. Each has enriched my life. One by one, these amazing encounters helped me to better understand and appreciate the fullness of life.

I offer these stories as an encouragement for each of us to look at life a little differently and to open ourselves to the possibilities of receiving blessings from people who may only share our lives for brief intervals.

I hope that you enjoy these stories. Perhaps they will help you to hear a message from someone whom you might otherwise not have heard. Maybe they will encourage you to open yourself to someone who needs a message that only you can give. Or, you may hear a story that touches your heart and strengthens you. Perhaps the realization that such encounters can happen in your life will lift your spirit.

So, here we go. Travel with me, and may you feel a little brighter for having taken the journey.

Keep Dreaming

As I walk up the stairs, I wonder, whose weary legs carry me? I enter the bathroom and begin the nightly ritual of brushing my teeth and washing my face. I pass the mirror and view a face that has grown old. I touch my head and no longer feel the full head of hair that once adorned it. For a moment, I wonder, is this really me?

I enter the bedroom and see a white-haired man, chest bare, who lies no longer in passionate wait for his beloved. Instead, he waits for the lights to dim, for soft music to play, and for sleep, perfect sleep, to overcome him.

Tonight, he gently touches my back, and memories of his touch flood my being.

As I close my eyes, I wonder how my mother felt at seventy-five. How many years did she live with only the occasional touch from daughters, sons-in-law, grandchildren, or great-grandchildren? I no longer question why her life ended in fantasies of elephants walking down stairways, or why the sound of joy rose from her less and less as the years passed by.

Mom lived with one man for nearly 75 years and birthed three daughters and a son, whom she barely met before the heavens swept him away. She lived nearly one-hundred and three years and is now one of the angels watching over us.

Today, I am seventy-five, and I often wonder what the remainder of my life holds. Will I continue searching for some unknown treasure to validate my existence? Will I become more and more a reflection of my mother's face? Will I look with longing as I watch my children and their children chart new roads to travel?

As I lie in bed, I quietly watch my beloved snore softly beside me. His belief in me has never wavered.

I slip out of bed and pass slowly down darkened hallways and light-less stairways. My mind is weary from questioning tomorrow, and yet it races, forbidding sleep to conquer.

Where will life take this restless seventy-five-year-old? Where do I want to go, what do I want to see, to explore, to conquer? Did time pass too quickly while I raised children or sat beside an aging mother who, as time passed, believed I was her mother? Is it too late now to open doors that have slowly closed before me?

What is that thing I want to explore, to conquer, to embrace? Surely it is more than death, which rubs its hands in anticipation of my arrival. Certainly, it is not to re-experience the passion I knew as a young woman.

What is it I long for? Do I have one more race to run? Am I like the old stallion standing at the starting gate, his legs saying, "this is it, old fellow; enjoy this last surge out of the gate?"

So, for me, what shall it be, a bucket list, a service project, or an unimagined joy that awaits me? Will I sit in a darkened house, writing alone, searching for the unknown, and praying there is a heaven – and if there is heaven, what will it be like to see all those beloveds who have gone home before me?

What am I seeking, why does the answer elude me over and over again? Will I grow old, never quite knowing if I have made a difference for having been here? Should I pray that my children and my children's children recognize that I loved them beyond measure?

I return to my bed and gaze at my sleeping darling, a man who made my journey more complete than I could have ever imagined. Does he know how much I have loved him? I have loved him like no other, despite and because of the hills and the valleys we traveled together.

Oh, what if anything, awaits my presence tomorrow? Even now, as my body aches and my heart seeks peace, should I not believe that I must boldly take each moment that is given to me, and mold it as only I can?

I need to sleep so that tomorrow I may rise to face another day – a day filled with challenges, wrapped in hope, and tied with dreams. Yes, even a seventy-five-year-old dreams, still longs to be of value, and still wants to believe that her presence can make a difference, even if just for a moment.

I sit on the bed and wonder how many others lie awake while asking themselves if there are other gifts to share or one more marvelous hill to climb? Surely, I am not alone in my wondering!

I lie down and feel sleep begin to gently flow through my body. I smile, knowing that whatever tomorrow offers, I will meet its challenge. I will overcome my doubts. I will give life all I have, believing that in giving, I am made whole. Perhaps I shall finish my stories.

REFLECTIONS

May you never stop dreaming,
for dreams are the key to a fulfilled life.

Two Men, One Sorrow

Riding the train offers many different opportunities, but seldom do they include solitude. However, Friday's Amtrak train from Princeton, New Jersey to New York City offered me the rarest of pleasures – a seat all to myself.

I nestled back against the headrest to relax and daydream. I took in the sounds that filled the car: the clanging of the wheels, and the soft hum of music flowing from headphones. The smells of food, mixed with body scents, invaded my nostrils, as people walked back and forth from the snack bar. I marveled at the constantly changing faces of fellow passengers as they entered and left the train.

As the train moved from the station, I became aware of a new smell. It was alcohol, and it flowed in from the seat behind me. I shifted my body in an attempt to avoid the poignant scent of stale alcohol. But it did not work. Then, a hand tapped my shoulder, and a voice asked what the next stop would be. As I turned to face the man who had touched my shoulder, he asked, to my surprise, if he could sit in the empty seat next to mine. Before I could answer, he settled in beside me.

Before he finished sitting down, he began to tell me that his wife had recently left him and had taken their two children. He admitted that he had a drinking problem and that he didn't know what to do or where to go to for help. He shared with me that he had lost his job due to his drinking and that he felt helpless. I told him that he had just taken the first step to getting help: admitting that alcohol was the root of his problem.

I asked him what he wanted. He said, without hesitation, that he wanted his family back. I wondered whether he was willing to work hard to make that happen. I told him he must be prepared for his wife's being unwilling to try again, despite his efforts to change. He said that no matter what, he wanted to feel better and to be able, at least, to see his kids.

I talked to him about Alcoholics Anonymous (AA) and ALANON for his family, and he said that he didn't have insurance. He was surprised when I told him that all he needed was a desire to stop drinking. He told me he wanted to try, and I gave him the name of a program in New Jersey he could contact. We talked about how difficult it would be to put his life back in order, just as thousands of others had successfully done. We talked about not giving up, but rather giving in to the reality that he had to stop drinking.

When his stop came, he leaned over, kissed my cheek, said thanks, and left the train. I felt overwhelmed by his story and yet hopeful that he would find help.

A nap seemed like a great idea. As I settled back to think about what had just happened, a voice from across the aisle startled me.

"Excuse me, may I talk to you? My wife is going to leave me because of my drinking."

Before I could respond, the seat next to me was occupied once again. Another fellow traveler was telling me about his problem with alcohol. I listened, found out where he lived, and told him how to find an AA meeting close to his home. I encouraged him to call immediately and to share our conversation with his wife, hoping that he might avoid the tragedy of losing his family. We talked about the reality that there are no quick fixes and no easy solutions, but that, one day at a time, he could find his way back to a place of wholeness, alcohol-free.

We were near the end of our conversation when the conductor announced my stop. As I stood, my seat companion rose and embraced me. He thanked me for listening and for offering him some advice and comfort.

How amazing! First, a jobless and simply dressed man told me his story. Then a well-dressed and employed man shared a nearly identical story.

I left the train, lifted by talking with two men who may have come from "different sides of the track," but each headed for similar destruction. My heart rejoiced, for I had been blessed to share a little of myself with two struggling travelers. I prayed then and continue to pray that our meeting was a blessing to each man and perhaps, in time, to two families.

REFLECTIONS

*Let us see the potential for growth and change,
even among those who appear lost.*

The Purse

My encounters while riding public transportation fill me with the wonder of life. I love the magic of sitting and watching people move about the bus. Some are loaded down with bundles of all types and sizes. Older folks walk gingerly, afraid of falling as the bus moves forward. School children talk and laugh, oblivious to others around them. Young mothers juggle babies and strollers. People with all manner of physical challenges try to hold on as they scan the isles for empty seats.

I feast on the visual mosaic of people flowing through the bus and the symphony of sounds: children laughing, babies crying, people coughing, and the bus door swooshing as it opens and closes. This ménage of sights and sounds fills my being sometimes to the point of distraction, and even forgetfulness.

Today was one of those days. As I walked away from the bus, near Washington's Union Station, I realized, too late, that my purse remained on the bus, and the bus was starting to move. Panic rose in my chest, but I then remembered that since this was the last stop, the bus would linger for a while on the upper level of the station.

As I hurried up the ramp, I noticed a young man walking swiftly from the bus. I quickened my steps to speak to the bus driver before he closed the door. I felt confident that my purse would still be there because it appeared that everyone but the young man had gotten off at the previous stop.

The bus driver frowned when I told him what had happened. He mentioned that a young man had asked if he could ride to the top of the ramp, and on arrival, he had exited through the back door. The driver told me to look for my purse and that he hoped it had not been taken. To my horror, the purse was gone.

I thanked the driver, and he drove off, leaving me on the empty platform. I turned to walk away and noticed a young man standing on the other side of the ramp. I smiled as I approached him and spoke with all the confidence I could muster,

"I bet you saw my purse and picked it up, planning to take it to lost and found."

Then, in a lighthearted manner, I said he had probably been embarrassed to carry a lady's handbag and had decided to tuck it under his coat. With that, I extended my hand and said, "Thanks so much." I told him what can seem like a blessing to one person could be a horrible loss to another.

The young man mumbled inaudibly as he opened his jacket and handed me my purse. I looked directly at this young person and said, "Let me give you something for returning my bag to me."

I began to open my purse, but the young man turned and ran. Suddenly, I felt isolated, and I quickly left the area.

As I walked away, my thoughts raced. I realized that I had never felt afraid of this young man, though the look of confusion in his eyes remained with me. Perhaps he had learned, in his short life, to take what seemed to be there for the taking. Maybe, my hand reaching out to him helped him to "do the right thing." Or, perhaps others in his life had rarely expected goodness from him.

I walked away from this encounter, wondering what events in this young man's life had led to the emptiness that I witnessed in his eyes. I wondered what emotions had raced through him as he left the bus with my handbag. I felt sadness for this young person and thought that what seemed like a tragedy to me, might have felt like a blessing to him. I reminded myself that we often judge others without ever trying to understand their perception of our shared experience.

REFLECTIONS

Let us always remain open to the reality that life is not the same for each of us; that our personal histories play a role in our perceptions of the same event. May we remember that what may seem like a loss to one may appear to be a blessing to someone else.

Granny's Love

As I stood on the elevated train platform, I wondered why it always seemed to feel cooler or hotter there than at ground level. From the platform, the rest of the world appeared relatively far away. But the sounds from the street and the smells of that hot summer day reminded me that I was just a few steps from the world below.

I read my book to relax while waiting for my train, but soon became distracted by my fellow travelers who came and went in a steady stream. Why had I come so early, I wondered? But in truth, I knew very well that an important part of all my journeys is the waiting and the watching, becoming connected in some small way with my fellow travelers. Finally, I sat, determined to wait patiently for my train.

I glanced around the train platform and noticed a young woman standing nearby. She was overdressed for such a hot summer afternoon. She smiled shyly at me, even though her eyes looked sad. I was touched by those sad eyes, and I returned her smile.

After a few minutes, the young lady came and sat beside me. We began to talk, first about the weather and then about her life. She told me that she was on her way to the funeral of her uncle, who had died from what she described as his "heart exploding." When she said that her uncle had been addicted to crack, I guessed that he had suffered a fatal heart attack.

This young woman was the mother of twins. She lived in an area riddled with drugs, but unlike many others in her neighborhood, she had not become an addict. She shared a story with me that seemed incredible. Yet there seemed no reason for her to lie to me, a stranger.

With downcast eyes, she confessed that her father had once shamed her into trying crack. He told her that she needed to come down from her "high horse" and realize that she wasn't better than everyone else. She was frightened, but she feared the loss of her father's love more than she feared trying crack.

I was stunned that a father would do such a thing, but I also wondered why, on this hot summer day, this young woman would share her story with me. As she talked, I recognized her need to share her experience with someone, and today, I happened to be there. She spoke of drugs and the horrors she had seen. She told me that her Granny was the only person close to her who was also drug-free.

After this experience with her father, she knew that she could no longer stay where she was living and asked her grandmother if she and the children could move in with her. She smiled as she related her Granny's response. "Yes, child, you and those babies just come right here."

As I listened, I realized that this young person's life was a constant struggle. Today, she was burying her uncle, but she had lost other loved ones, even while they lived.

I told her how blessed she was to have a Granny who was willing to open both heart and home to her and her children. We talked about her responsibility, not only to her twins but also to herself. She told me that she had started going to Granny's church and had met some other young adults who were drug-free. I encouraged her to continue attending church and to think about trying to get some training to bring financial stability into her life.

She made me smile with funny stories about her precious babies, and I told her that while parenting is never easy, the blessings were immeasurable. It seemed as though only minutes had passed when her train arrived. We hugged and said goodbye.

As her train left the platform, I realized why on that particular day, I had arrived nearly forty minutes early for mine.

REFLECTIONS

Bless all the Grannies who are trying to help their children's children and send light to all the children who are struggling to find their way.

The Glance

The sun's rays eluded me on that chilly April morning. I day-dreamed of brighter days and a hot cup of coffee. I reminded myself to relax and to enjoy the momentary silence rather than spend my time fretting over the weather.

Unwinding, listening to the sound of the birds, and enjoying the smell of the approaching spring comforted me and lessened my feeling of loneliness. I was grateful for the quiet moment, as I knew that soon the bus stop would be filled with fellow travelers whose sounds and motions would become a part of my journey.

I sat alone on the cold bus stop seat. I looked up and into the face of a driver in a passing car. He looked at me, too, as though he recognized me. For a moment, his expression made me wonder whether I knew this young man.

Within minutes, this same young man walked toward me. I saw the sadness in his eyes, and his shuffle made his youthful body seem much older. He stopped and sat beside me. I wondered where and why he had left his car. Had I imagined that this was the same person who had driven past me?

Then the young man spoke softly. "I stopped because when I looked at you, I knew that you would be willing to talk to me."

Before I could respond, he began his soul-wrenching story. The weight of his sorrow over-whelmed the space between us. He told me that his wife and their unborn son had recently died. I turned to look directly at him as he talked. Several buses came and went while he spoke of a life that overflowed with pain. He lowered his head into his hands and said that he could not understand why these things had happened to him.

I wondered what I might say to lessen his pain. I asked him about his relationship with God. He told me he was a Christian, but that he had stopped going to church. When I suggested that he might be angry with God, he grew silent. I shared with him my belief that God never promised bad things would not engulf us, but that He would never leave us alone. This seemed the only response to his sorrow.

I reminded him that in his time of deepest pain, he was not alone, that God was present and loved him. The young man nodded and spoke of his love for his wife. I encouraged him to hold on to those precious memories, but to not let himself become destroyed by grief and anger.

As the conversation continued, he said that he needed to go back to church. I smiled and shared my belief that people would welcome him back with open arms. We sat quietly for a time, and when he got up to leave, we gently squeezed one another's hands, and I wished him peace.

REFLECTIONS

Let us be grateful for the blessing that allows two strangers to share a moment of pain and a message of hope!

Words Remembered

When the doorbell or the telephone rings late at night, I get alarmed, because I assume the late-night caller will bring bad news. This particular winter night was no exception. When the doorbell rang at 11 PM, I nervously opened the door to a young woman who had previously been a co-worker of mine.

She was very special to me, and despite my trying over the past few years to stay in touch, we had not seen one another in a long time. Her late-night presence heightened my anxiety.

The last time we met was over lunch. She did not look well. I asked whether I could be supportive in some way. She replied that she was fine, but that she and her husband were having some problems. He had lost his job, and they, in turn, had lost their townhouse and had moved in with her parents. She assured me that things were getting better, but it was not at all clear to me how they were improving.

Tonight, she stood in my doorway, looking unkempt and older than her age. Her daughter was sick, she said, and she needed twenty dollars to buy medicine. As I looked and listened, my heart ached for this young woman. She displayed clear signs of someone abusing drugs, and I knew she was in serious trouble. We had talked about drug abuse in the past, but only concerning her husband.

I told her that I did not have twenty dollars and asked which pharmacy would be open so late. She ignored my question and disengaged herself from any further discussion. She told me that her mother was waiting in the car and that she had to go.

Several days after that incident, I went to her mother's home. There I found my friend looking even thinner and more unkempt than she had appeared at my door. She was surprised to see me. I wanted to talk with her about her possible involvement with drugs, so I asked her if we could speak privately.

She listened to my concerns and my offer of help. I told her she needed to find a way to put her life back together, if not for herself, then for her children who needed her desperately. I told her that I and others loved her, but she needed to fall in love with herself.

She listened, but protested that she did not have a drug problem. She insisted that things had fallen apart because she and her husband were both unemployed. I took her hand and reminded her that God loved her. I told her that she had to learn to love herself and believe in His love for her. As I prepared to leave, I told her that if she ever needed me, she knew where to find me.

I left with a heavy heart, convinced that this young woman was caught in a web of lies and self-deceit that too often become the mainstay for those who are addicted.

Over the next few years, I called her periodically at her mother's house, but the conversations were difficult, and eventually, I stopped calling. My last words to her were that I loved her.

Nearly four years later, on an evening in early Spring, my friend surprised me with a phone call.

"I just wanted to tell you that I have been drug-free for two years," she said.

I began to cry, assuring her that my tears were those of joy and that my heart rejoiced for her. She told me that she had not been able to forget the pain in my eyes the last time we met. She said that she had remembered my message that she had to learn to love herself. She thanked me for my willingness to confront her behavior and for my love. She went on to say that she had fallen in love with herself, that she was attending church, and in a healthy relationship.

I was filled with joy and a sense of reaffirmation that loving someone is never a wasted effort. Love may not always be received when it is offered, but that does not diminish the importance of sharing it. I hung up the telephone with a joyful heart and an uplifted spirit because one who had been lost was found.

REFLECTIONS

May those who are lost find their way safely home. Let us remember that as long as one person is struggling, our work on earth is not done.

Choices

Train stations have always fascinated me, with their throngs of people hurrying here and there.

For me, waiting for trains is a blessing, rarely a nuisance. While waiting, I can collect my thoughts. Slowly, I become a part of a fuller world than my daily life usually offers. Waiting allows me to recognize that all types of possibilities are available when surrounded by so many people. In train stations, I imagine where all the people are going, and I feel more aware and open to life's boundless possibilities.

This day, as I waited in Grand Central Station, was no exception. I was somewhat overwhelmed by the number and variety of people moving all around me. Families hurried to catch their trains. Small groups of passengers gathered periodically around the incoming board, fearing they had missed their connections. Homeless people scavenged for scraps of food left behind and for change in telephone wells. Some people seemed uncertain about where they were or where they were going. The great hall was filled with a melody of different languages fusing, yet not quite in harmony. Some of these travelers shared intimacies of hurried goodbyes or long welcoming embraces.

As I was waiting for my train, a young woman sat down beside me. It would have been hard not to notice her provocative dress and her constant motion, even while she sat.

Shortly, another young woman, similarly dressed, came to her and asked quietly how things were going. The first woman said, "OK," and that she had almost reached the amount she needed that night. After some small talk, the second young woman left me with my original companion.

After a few moments, I spoke to her in a low voice and told her that I had overheard her conversation with her friend and that it had troubled me. She glared at me, her eyes empty and angry, and asked what business it was of mine. I replied that experience had taught me that the loss of one life affected the universe. I told her that if she had to work the streets, she needed to protect herself as much as she could.

Somewhat less belligerently, she asked why it mattered to me. I replied that the loss of her life would diminish mine. I told her that she, like me, had a gift to share with the world and prayed that she would have the opportunity to discover hers.

I told her that even though we might not ever see each other again that, from time to time, I would include her in my prayers.

My words surprised us both. She looked confused but

continued to listen as I told her she was a part of my life and I a part of hers. For this brief moment, our lives had touched, and there was a message that I needed to share... that God loved her. He loved her no matter what she did, and that I loved her, too, because, like me, she was a child of God. Perhaps if our life circumstances had been different, I could have been she and she, I.

We sat silently for a short time. Suddenly she stood up and said, "Thanks, lady." Then she walked away.

REFLECTIONS

*May all the young people who are lost hear
the message that they too are loved.*

Mother and Child

We love our cars. We can jump in them at any time and travel directly and efficiently to pre-determined destinations.

Buses are different. They continually stop and start to let off and take on passengers. They are also filled with adventure: a simple bus ride can remind us that life is constantly changing.

Riding the bus offers a fresh look at life. The world on a bus, different from the world of passenger cars, is fuller and more intrusive. It offers boundless opportunities to be touched, figuratively and literally, by those around us.

This day, as I rode the bus that travels the Georgia Avenue corridor from Washington, DC to Silver Spring, the smell of french fries taunted my nostrils. That aroma and the "No Eating Allowed" sign reminded me that many of these passengers run from the fast-food lines to the bus lines, without a moment to spare.

As I sat on the bus reading *Essence,* I sensed the young girl who sat beside me. She was perhaps sixteen or seventeen years old and held an adorable baby. The little boy was no more than six or seven months old. They appeared to be mother and child. As I watched these two "children," I observed the baby pulling at mommy's brightly colored beads. Each time he grabbed at her beads, the young mother slapped his hands and told him not to touch. But he continued to reach for them. Each time his mother slapped his hand, the infant seemed surprised and cried out softly.

After watching for a while, I turned towards the young woman and smiled. "Is he your little boy? He is fascinated by your beads."

Her expression was flat as she returned my gaze. "I can't have anything that is just mine anymore," she replied.

This lovely young mother, still a child herself, was burdened by anger and sadness for the responsibility of this new life and, perhaps, for her lost youth.

Then I asked the young woman if she would like to read my *Essence.* Without the slightest hesitation, she took the magazine and asked me to hold her baby. She handed me her child, a beautiful, inquisitive little one, took my magazine, and, to my amazement, asked if she could go to the back of the bus to read. Before I could respond, this woman-child, smiling broadly, and clutching my magazine, slipped away to an empty seat in the rear of the bus.

For the next thirty minutes, this young girl lost herself in the wonders of *Essence* while the baby and I cuddled and cooed. As I held the precious baby boy, I was filled with sadness for this young mommy and her little child. Their journey together had barely begun, and already mommy was overwhelmed. She was willing to leave her son with a stranger to have a solitary moment for herself. Empathy and grief filled my heart. Surely her decision to go to the back of the bus did not reflect a lack of love for her son, but merely a teenager's need to be free to dream.

I could only hope that my willingness to share, what might have felt like a heavy load, was a reminder that she was not alone.

Through the years, I have thought often of these two "children" and have prayed that someone was able to give each of them the nurturing and love they both deserved and needed.

REFLECTIONS

Let us find a way to encourage young people to make choices that open doors to self-fulfillment.

Let us guide those who may have stumbled to believe that new beginnings are possible.

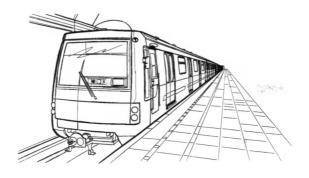

The Shuttle

There is a wonderful underground shuttle that carries passengers between Grand Central Station and Penn Station, New York. I am amazed by the number of people who use the shuttle. They all move swiftly and seem to go unnoticed by one another. Their silence offers poignant testimony that these travelers remain strangers to each other, even as they pass day after day within hand's reach of one another. As I stood, waiting for the shuttle, I wondered how often in our haste do we pass one another and miss opportunities to share ourselves, if only for a brief moment.

The shuttle would take me to Penn Station. There I would connect with New Jersey Transit and return to New Brunswick, where I was conducting a class on cultural diversity.

As I waited for the shuttle, a young woman approached and asked how to get to Penn Station. When I replied that

I was going there, she asked if she and her friend could go with me. She added that they were in New York City for the Gay Pride March and that it was their first time using the New York subway system.

During our passage to Penn Station, I learned that both, after coming out, had been disowned by their parents. They acknowledged their sorrow, but their words fell short of the pain conveyed on their faces.

I wondered how a parent disowns a child. There is nothing that either of my children could do that would make me walk away from them. Their decisions or actions might sadden or anger me, but I could never remove them from my life.

I told these two young women that I was a mother and that sometimes parents become blind to those things that are truly important, such as loving others, especially our children, as we want to be loved. Sometimes even parents get lost in a maze of "isms, shoulds, and shouldn'ts."

We talked about keeping open the lines of communication, if not by telephone, then perhaps through letters. I suggested they send notes to their parents, to share the little joys that filled their daily lives and their struggles as well. Perhaps these notes could help their parents to see their lives as a textured tapestry of experiences, encompassing far more than their sexual orientation.

I told them that if the bridge between them and their parents could not be crossed, then they might try to find "parents" whom they could "adopt" as their own. Most of all, I told them they needed to believe that they were worthy of being loved. I shared my personal belief that they were and would always be loved by God.

We talked about acceptance and the need for all of us to find a way to respect one another and to stop judging.

Before long, we reached Penn Station, and it was time to say goodbye. The two young women and I embraced, and off they went. I watched as they walked away. Silently, I prayed that others would be kind to them and see them as two beautiful young people who had fallen in love.

REFLECTIONS

Let us remain open to others, even to passing strangers. When our lives touch, even briefly, let us remember to love others as we have been loved.

Cloth Diapers

The ringing of the telephone awakened my husband and me with a start. I picked up the phone, surprised to hear Pearl's voice. Pearl was a young woman and a single parent of three children whom my husband and I mentored. My heartbeat quickened as I feared something had happened to one of her little ones. My pulse raced as I struggled to sit up in bed and turn on the light.

Pearl was frantic. She said that the baby was wet and that she was out of pampers. She was frustrated, and I felt drained. I knew that Pearl had two dozen cloth diapers at hand. We had given them to her in an unsuccessful attempt to encourage her to reduce household expenses by eliminating the cost of disposable diapers. We had talked to her at length about the expense of disposable diapers for parents on very limited incomes, but Pearl had decided to use them anyway.

I tried to relax and to not sound annoyed at this mother

of three, who had awoken us in the middle of the night. I reminded her of the cloth diapers we had given her. Pearl said that she did not know how to put them on the baby and that she had a diaper in front of her, but she didn't know what to do with it. I was astonished that this young mother, who was struggling financially, had never tried to use a cloth diaper.

I had to think for a moment while I retrieved forty-year-old memories of diapering my children. Once I visualized the shape of the diaper, I was able to talk her through this new experience. Finally, she said she had it on. Thank goodness we had included diaper pins!

I was ready to hang up the phone and to go back to sleep when Pearl said she didn't think that she should use cloth diapers. She said that the hospital used disposable ones. She believed that they were better for babies than the cloth ones because the hospital would only use what was best.

As she spoke, I realized the disservice we have done to thousands of struggling parents by suggesting that only disposable diapers will do. What a horrible message for parents whose limited financial resources are already overtaxed. I reassured Pearl that the baby would be fine, but that she needed to change the cloth diapers frequently. I told her that if she washed and rinsed them thoroughly, they would be excellent for her baby. I reminded her that she was very fortunate that she had access to a washing machine and dryer in her apartment.

When we hung up, I felt less annoyed with her and more frustrated with myself for my lack of sensitivity. In our previous discussions about disposable diapers, I had never asked why she thought they were better. I realized that Pearl, no different from most parents, wanted what she thought was best for her baby. Doesn't the hospital use only the best?

This experience reminded me that we should carefully consider the messages that we give to one another. Do we recognize the dilemmas we may create when we imply that there is only one right choice and that other choices mark us as less loving, less responsible parents? As we attempt to be supportive of others, whose lives are different from our own, we should question the implied values we impose on them. It is effortless to suggest that "those people" use disposable diapers, or engage in other behaviors because they are lazy, or financially irresponsible. But we must consider the possibility that they may be trying to emulate a model that was presented to them as "best."

REFLECTIONS

May we expand our minds and open our hearts to others, and remember that people are more than the decisions they make or the labels we place on them.

The Set Table

The young woman whom I hoped to mentor drew me in immediately. It was impressive that she would let me, a stranger, into her life to help her find a way to make life more manageable for herself and her children.

The first time I visited Pat's home, I noticed that the dining table was set nicely for dinner. How wonderful, I thought, that she and her children sat together for meals.

During that visit, I learned that her oldest child had been diagnosed with Attention-Deficit/Hyperactivity Disorder and that his medication helped only marginally. She told me that no matter how much she punished him, he just didn't listen and that things were not getting better at home or in school.

As we continued to talk about her son's behavior, I suggested using a reward system rather than punishment. I told her that rewarding a child for good behavior often worked better than punishing the child for inappropriate behavior.

We talked about a method that would allow him to earn rewards for specific improved behaviors. She seemed really excited about the possibility of her son being able to move in a positive direction. We discussed our meeting the following week when the kids were not present and practicing this new method.

She was also frustrated that her children did not take care of their things. We talked about the need to teach children how to share, how to value things, theirs and others, and how to build on their strengths. We discussed appropriate age-related expectations and how children learn through observation and consistency. We talked of the need to spend appropriate time and energy on her children. We explored how children did not automatically know, but had to be taught, what was acceptable behavior. We shared experiences around the difficulties of raising children as single parents.

Over several hours, we talked and laughed and agreed that we would like to spend time together. I was deeply moved that my husband and I would have a chance to become a part of this family's support network. The time to leave came all too soon.

As I put on my coat, I mentioned the dining room table and how nicely it was set. Her reply amazed me.

She smiled and said that it always looked that way because she never let the children eat at the table. She said that they ate on the floor because they were messy. She added, rather firmly, that she was not going to let them destroy her beautiful things.

With a sense of sadness, I pictured mom in a chair, while her children ate on the floor. How would they learn to use and enjoy the beauty around them unless they were taught? Perhaps one day, mother and childern would eat together at this lovely table.

REFLECTIONS

As we embrace others whose lives and experiences are different from our own, may we love unselfishly, listen with caring ears, respond with gentle words, and try to understand, without judgment, the decisions they make.

Mom's Elephants

Mom had reached nearly 100 years old and was doing fairly well. However, she could no longer take care of her basic needs, and she had not been able to walk for several years. She would sit in her chariot, while others pushed!

At this point in her life, Mom was not overly talkative, but occasionally she could be chatty. While my sister, Myrtle, and I provided ongoing care for Mom, her sons-in-law had a special gift of engaging her in memories of days gone by. One son-in-law, Bill, who lived nearby, made sure that she ate her lunch every day. Another "sister", Norma, stayed with Mom while we took our annual week-long vacation. What extraordinary gifts of love!

One afternoon, as Mom and I sat together, she kept looking beyond the television, rather than at it. Finally, I asked, "Mom, what are you looking at?"

She smiled and said, "I'm watching the elephants walking down the stairs."

Elephants? I turned my head to look and said, "Wow, how many are there?"

Mom looked more intensely and finally said, "I don't know, but a lot."

Several minutes passed as together, mother and daughter watched the phantom elephants.

As we looked in the direction of the imaginary stairs, I realized that while those animals were not real to me, they were authentic to Mom. Not only did she see them, but for a few precious moments, those elephants brought Mom and me together. Those wonderful, fictitious elephants made Mom smile, and her smile brought sheer joy to me.

Mom and I sat quietly together, sharing her new world. It seemed that the longer I allowed myself to look through her eyes, the more calming our time together became. A peaceful wave passed through my being. If even just for a few moments, how wonderful it was to feel that my mother was once again, my teacher. She was showing me something that I would otherwise not have been able to see.

REFLECTIONS

Perhaps if we can share the vision of someone dear to us, though it may differ from our own, the reward may be greater than we could ever imagine. We may see both the beauty and the pain that they experience. If we are open to their experiences, our time together may be enriched.

So, to all the daughters and sons who are intent on their reality and afraid to enter their parent's new world vision, try to pause for just a moment and enjoy the "elephants." May memories and love fill your spirit and give you peace.

Mahani

The day my husband, our two children, and I arrived in Zaire (the present-day Democratic Republic of the Congo), we were filled with excitement and apprehension.

Upon arrival, we entered the airport waiting area and were immediately enmeshed in a sea of people. We saw women adorned in colorful dresses and magnificent headpieces and heard men shouting in French and other languages that we had never before heard. Our eyes and ears struggled to take it all in. Everything and everyone seemed to be in a state of complete and utter confusion.

For a brief moment, I doubted the wisdom of what we had done – bringing our two children into a world that seemed so different from anything we had ever experienced.

We sauntered through a maze of people, feeling overwhelmed by the sights, sounds, and smells. Suddenly, someone called our names, and within seconds this wonderful African man smiled at us and invited us to follow him to a waiting car.

As we exited the airport, many people offered to carry our luggage. I moved swiftly, afraid of being left behind and paused only slightly to say "no thank you" to outstretched hands. I feared that my limited French might make me appear to be a rude guest in what was to be our home for the next three years. The ride from the airport to Kinshasa, the capital of Zaire, passed quickly. The sights entranced us along the way: people on bicycles, richly colored women's clothing, the roadside markets, and the smells of roasted meats.

One memory of that first night remains vivid. As we approached our new home, we saw a rather small man with the warmest smile standing in the doorway. This was Mahani, whom the embassy's hospitality unit had assigned to work in our house. Mahani soon became more than the man who helped to keep our home in order; he became our friend.

As days turned into months, Mahani not only cooked and cleaned for us, but he guided me in ways to survive our new experience. He taught me how to cover our heads from the hot African sun. He showed me how to cut hot peppers, not holding them in my hands, but by placing them on a cutting board.

Mahani did not speak English, and my French was limited; yet, we found a way to communicate. We shared common experiences and laughed together when we mis-used French or Lingala in our conversation.

One day, Mahani asked if his wife, Kabanga, could cultivate a small vegetable garden in our yard. I was delighted. We had more than enough space, and I could make a new friend.

The next day, Mahani brought his beautiful, tall, stately, and shy wife for me to meet. Kabanga spoke no French, and I did not speak her local language. Still, we began to work side by side in the garden. For several days, we dug, planted, and perspired together, communicating with our hands, our eyes, and our laughter.

One morning, as we were turning the soil, Kabanga pointed to a snake. I screamed and began to run. Kabanga ran behind me. She laughed and held the snake with her hoe. Mahani heard the uproar and came outside. He tried to explain that it was just a baby snake. I reasoned that a baby snake must have a mama and a daddy snake, so I put my gardening on hold until vegetables started to sprout. I can still hear Kabanga's laughter over my fear of the snake!

Months later, I learned that Mahani and his wife had been amazed that I would join her in working the garden. Often, I brought rice, sardines, and soda, and we had lunch together. It was hard for them to comprehend that *Madame* would work side by side in the dirt with a houseman's wife. I believe it was the beginning of a deeper relationship.

Often, while Kabanga worked in the garden, I sat outside near the garden and folded laundry or worked on other household chores. Occasionally, Kabanga would start to laugh, and I knew that she had seen a snake. Her joyful laughter was contagious. Sometimes we would laugh until tears filled our eyes.

One afternoon, I mentioned to Mahani that his wife was very beautiful. He agreed but said that she was too thin. I smiled and replied that I was too fat! His response puzzled me. He seemed so happy to hear this. Did Zairian men like fat women?

Later that day, when my husband returned home, Mahani was quick to congratulate him on the great news. It was then I realized that my comment in French to Mahani meant not that I was too fat, but that I was pregnant!

There are no words to express the surprise and honor we felt when Mahani and Kabanga invited our family to their home. He asked if he could take six glasses to his house for us to use when we visited, and I readily agreed.

It was rare for expatriates to be invited to the home of a person working in their house. In fact, during the three years we were in Zaire, I never once heard of such a thing.

Several weeks later, on a Saturday, our family dressed up and waited for Mahani to accompany us to his home. When we arrived, Mahani showed us where to park the car. Then we walked up what seemed like a small mountain to reach his home, a very small thatched structure on the side of a hill.

That afternoon we sat together on the ground outside his home, ate peanuts, and drank beer and sodas. This simple meal felt like a banquet fit for royalty. Our time was filled with laughter as we came together in the name of friendship. What an amazing day!

Mahani enriched our African experience. I shall forever treasure the memories of his friendship and support. How different our time would have been had I remained *Madame* and he, a nameless man who worked in our house.

REFLECTIONS

Let us open our minds and our hearts to others.
May we look beyond race, social & economic status,
gender orientation, and other labeling traps, so that
our lives may be enriched by embracing and being
embraced by all people.

The Unfinished Wedding Dress

To fully appreciate our present, we must sometimes rewind our memories and travel back to another time. Come with me to August 25, 1972, the day before my wedding and a day of imminent disaster.

I had come to my parents' house to try on my wedding dress, so Mom could make final adjustments. Mom was an excellent seamstress. She had made many of my clothes during my teen and early adult years. I was excited when she agreed to make my wedding dress. I had chosen the pattern and selected a light green color in a soft, flowing fabric.

I had not seen my dress since Mom cut out the pattern. With only one day to prepare, I was not concerned. In those days Mom rarely needed to make adjustments to anything she sewed.

I entered the house and found Mom in the kitchen. I smiled as she turned towards me and I told her I had come to try on my dress. Mom looked startled. She said she wasn't quite finished with it. She seemed uneasy as I followed her into her bedroom.

Then she began to pull out pieces of green material from the bottom drawer of her dresser, and I realized the reason for her anxiety. She had not begun to sew my dress. The material was just as I had last seen it. She had done nothing since cutting the material for my dress!

Mom stood mute; she looked at the floor. She could not explain why she had not completed my dress. I wondered what was going on in her head. Had her fears of this marriage rendered her incapable of making my dress? It would take a miracle for me to find a nice, inexpensive dress at 5 PM on the day before my wedding. Was God giving me a sign that this marriage should not take place?

Suddenly, Mom began to apologize, and I, not knowing what to say, burst into tears. I did not understand how this could have happened. I knew Mom was ambivalent about my wedding, but how could she forget my dress?

We were startled when a dear friend peeked into the room and asked if everything were alright. Holding back my hysteria, I told her that Mom had not made my dress. Without raising an eyebrow or her voice, she told me not to worry. Not to worry! What was she thinking?

To my amazement, this friend went immediately into action. She made several calls and soon three women appeared at the door, sewing machines in tow. These marvelous women transformed my parents' dining room into a seamstress station and worked their magic over the next several hours. I watched in amazement as they turned pieces of green material into my wedding dress. Stitch by stitch, it became more beautiful than I had ever imagined.

My dress symbolized all the love and hard work undertaken by the hands of loving friends. Their chatter and laughter, more melodious than any orchestra, overcame my hopelessness and filled my spirit with joy.

The following afternoon, as I walked out into my parents' garden, where treasured friends and family had gathered, I felt nestled in a cocoon of love. I saw my parents standing among friends. Their eyes glistened with tears as they watched their youngest daughter marry for a second time. Surely, their joy for me overcame the anxiety they felt. I imagined that their hearts overflowed with hopes that this marriage would fulfill my dreams.

Peter and I stood under a fragrant trellis of wild flowers, picked by friends and two nieces. Hand in hand, we faced each other and recited the vows we had written together. We vowed to love one another and my two children from a previous marriage. Our thirteen-year-old niece stood with us and coached us whenever we hesitated in reciting our vows.

After the ceremony, Peter and I walked, hand in hand, smiling broadly at friends and family as we moved to another area of the garden. There, we shared a delicious meal created under the careful guidance of my dad and prepared by the loving hands of my mom, sisters and other family members.

Peter and I kept the vows we made to our children, and thirty-eight years later, they reciprocated in a most extraordinary way, when the children announced they wanted to adopt their dad! Over the previous years, Peter had always been the children's financial, emotional, and spiritual dad, but he had not legally adopted them. As the years passed, he was just "dad." Adoption never entered our minds.

How magnificent for this wonderful man to have his adult children, who had children of their own, want to be able to say, "My Dad," void of any limitations. They said it best: thirty-eight years before, he had chosen them. Now, they were choosing him.

When the legal documents were completed, the "children," Peter, and I went before the judge. We were accompanied by our children's spouses, our grandchildren and the lawyer who handled the adoption. After reviewing legal paperwork and asking a few questions, the judge declared us a "legal family." The judge smiled and said what a pleasure it was to meet such an unusual family. She said that it was her first time to have adult children come before her, with no other motive than to publicly affirm their love for their father. She said this was truly a case she would remember with joy.

The children's attorney also shared his delight at being a part of such a rare occasion. I wept with gratitude for all we had become, not just that day, but over the years.

Peter and I overflowed with joy as we left the courtroom with our daughter, her husband, and their daughter; our son, his wife, and their two children. Every prayer for unity that Peter and I had prayed, every sacrifice this remarkable man had made, and every gesture of love he had bestowed upon our children had not been missed by them. This man among men, who had never once hesitated to be the father he vowed to be, was honored that day in a way that one might experience only in a dream.

Peter, who first was my darling, easily became an incredible father who is, and will forever be, treasured and adored.

And what about me? My dream of a family that would remain united forever came true. Forty-seven years later, Peter - my lover, my friend, my husband - is now not only a father but a grandfather, who remains the joy of my life.

I remember that day, now so many years ago, when my dress was still in pieces, and our wedding ceremony just hours away. The unfinished dress was not a bad omen. It was just one of those moments in life when we must choose a path to follow. If we let fear and doubt possess us, we risk missing a lifetime of wonderful blessings.

REFLECTIONS

*May life's stumbling blocks never overwhelm
our dreams.*

Let us always remain grateful for family and friends.

The Socks

I was exhausted after completing Mom's nightly rituals. I brushed her teeth, made sure her nightgown was pulled down, put on her mesh hair net, and tucked her bedding under the mattress.

The last task was to give Mom two squares of chocolate, a special nightly treat. Regardless of who put her to bed, whether the staff or a family member, Mom got her treat. When she finished the chocolate, I leaned over her bed, kissed her forehead, told her I loved her, and turned off the bedside light.

When I reached her bedroom door, Mom spoke, "my socks; you didn't take off my socks."

I paused, knowing in my heart I had not forgotten. I went back over to her bed, untucked her bedding, reached down, and felt her naked feet. I said, "Mom," as I lifted her so she could see for herself, "there are no socks on your feet."

After she looked for herself, I rearranged the linens under her mattress. "Don't tell me my socks are off when they are still on my feet," she mumbled. I took a deep breath and refrained from responding.

Mom and the socks saga continued for the rest of her life. As time went on, I would say each night: "Good night, Mom. I love you, and your socks are in the hamper."

Mom continued to fret about her socks. Tension built as I left each night with a sense of failure and sadness. The nightly sock routine drained me.

One evening, as I was leaving, the night nurse asked if I was OK. I began to cry and told her about the socks. She smiled gently and said, "tomorrow night, when you leave her, stand outside her door and see how quickly she relaxes and goes to sleep."

The next night, I took the nurse's advice and waited by the door. Within three minutes, Mom was sound asleep. That night, I ate one donut on my way to my sister's home, instead of my usual two.

Had someone told me that a pair of nonexistent socks could create such pain, sadness, and, yes, guilt, I would not have believed it. Eventually, I learned that the sensation of socks probably was related to poor circulation and some anxiety, which created a feeling of tightness around Mom's ankles and feet.

I also came to realize that no explanation of why Mom felt she was wearing socks would diminish her anxiety. This was the journey she was on, one that logic did not often assuage. I had to learn more compassion and to love this new

Mom unconditionally, to be the daughter that she needed at that point in her life.

Today, I recognize that an increased understanding of the changes that may occur in the mind, body, and spirit as one ages might have made my heart beat a little slower and my stomach a little less knotted.

REFLECTIONS

*As parents grow older, may adult children develop
a greater understanding of the aging process.*

*May they be free to meet their parents on their new
journey and travel with them, even if ever so briefly.*

Forty-Eight Years
and Still Adored

Early in our relationship, Peter and I recognized that a successful marriage would require defining our independence and decision-making process. We believed that we would need strong communication skills because our children would need consistent messages.

For us, marriage would create a union not of two but four. If we decided to marry, we would begin our lives together with my two young children from a previous marriage.

After two years with much time spent as a foursome and countless hours of conversations, our love guided us to marry. In our first year, we made a major decision. I took a seven- day trip to Spain with a group of female friends and left the parenting to Peter.

I asked my parents to call, but also to allow Peter and his new children the space to bond. I believed that to become a family, the children needed to know that they could depend on daddy. They needed to feel that they could rely on both parents.

I trusted in the rightness of this decision but was uneasy nonetheless. My children were nine and seven years old and had been the center of my world since birth.

Leaving them and going out of the country meant placing my complete trust in my husband, the man they now called daddy. Remember, in 1973, there were no cell phones. I flew off to Spain, trusting in Peter's love not only of me but of my children.

I returned from Spain, eager to reclaim my place in the family unit. I heard how great daddy's boiled chicken tasted. BOILED CHICKEN? I listened to stories about daddy making bread and how they had all climbed onto the bed, ate hot homemade bread with butter and jelly, and watched television.

My momentary feelings of displacement paled in light of the joy I felt listening to their happy voices. My husband and children had bonded. They had become parent and children. No stepdad, just daddy.

As Peter and I forged ahead in our new life, we realized that communication was the key to our family survival. We spent hours talking, rehashing, learning to live, not only as a couple but as a family of four individuals, each with very strong personalities.

We learned that we had to function as a team. We had to speak in one voice to give the children the security and the confidence they needed to believe in this new union.

First, I had to share the children with this man for them to understand that it was alright for them to share themselves with him. Not only would they listen to my words, but to the silent messages that never passed unnoticed.

We laughed, we struggled, and sometimes we cried, but we always believed that as hard as it got as a family, it would be that much harder to divide us.

Together the four of us built an unbreakable bond. We trusted, loved, and got angry; and through it all, our caring and commitment deepened.

As our new family bonds grew stronger one of our biggest challenges was connecting with Peter's parents. Our marriage was very difficult for them to accept, for several reasons. Among them, his parents were Catholic, and he had married a divorced Methodist and the mother of two.

Though Peter's parents' failure to accept the children and me was hurtful, I also tried to understand. My parents had time to get to know Peter, to watch the four of us blend, while Peter's parents had refused to attend our wedding or have any contact with us. They only had their fear and anger to hold on to.

During our first year of marriage, I decided to send newsletters about our family to Peter's parents. I shared updates on what Peter was doing and things about the children and myself. I never received a response. All I could do was believe that they would read my messages and begin to see us as a part of their son's life.

Nearly two years of sending family updates passed when one night, we received a call from Peter's mother. She called to invite us to Thanksgiving dinner at their home. We were overjoyed but decided that going for dessert might be a gentler start and perhaps not too overwhelming for any of us.

When we arrived on Thanksgiving Day, our son went through the door first. Upon seeing Peter's dad, he opened his arms and said, "Hi grandpa!"

Peter and I froze. We realized that in all our discussions about how to behave, we had not told the children what to call Peter's parents.

Peter's father looked at our son with a smile and said, "you must be Willie." He then looked up and, with that same warm smile, said to our daughter, "you must be Dena. Welcome."

"Let the children lead them," raced from my head to my heart. At that moment, our extended family life began.

Though Peter's parents are now deceased, as are mine, we were blessed, many, many times over, by their presence in our lives. I received the unforgettable gift of having Peter's mother apologize for not attending our wedding.

Before his father died, he thanked me for the notes and for giving him back his son. These were powerful moments, never to be forgotten.

How often, over the years, have I remembered the scripture "do unto others as you would have them do unto you." It took so little time to write those newsletters. Yet, each note helped to bridge the gap and allowed us to have not just one, but two sets of parents. Both loved us and reminded us of the tremendous power and the gift of family.

As you read our story, I imagine that you formed some type of image of how we might look. Was Peter tall with blond hair, did I have red hair and freckles? Well, I am about 5'6" tall, with dark brown hair, a full-figure, and a brown-skinned body reflective of my African-American heritage. Peter is about 6' tall, medium build, with gorgeous blue eyes and a fair complexion, which is a reflection of his Irish-American background.

While this racial difference should not go unmentioned, it does not define us. Not unlike thousands of other couples who fell in love, our love was and remains the salient descriptor of who we are.

Today, it is heart-warming to see so many blended families who are comfortable being themselves, working hard, enjoying their children, and being the best parents they can be.

I continue to believe that being a blended family requires a commitment to recognize and celebrate each person and her/his racial/ethnic/gender and cultural identity. Like most couples, our union was never a political or social justice statement, but a reflection of our love.

Recently, at seventy-five years old, Peter and I decided that we needed to begin to prepare for the time when one of us will have to leave the other. We made provisions for our cremains to someday be co-mingled in one urn.

As we walked away from the cemetery office, I found myself looking at this man, whom I still adore, and thought how blessed we have been.

This story could have ended so differently or never have

begun. Fear could have made the journey seem over-whelming, the road too rocky, the climb too steep, but love made it impossible to walk away from one another.

What a journey nearly forty-eight years together has blessed us with, and however many more await us, no one can say. Yet, when the time comes to say farewell to one another, may we have the courage to say goodbye, knowing that we let love be our guide.

Epilogue

Dear Reader,

The stories I have shared with you are simple ones. They are stories about how we can touch, even briefly, each other's lives.

As you close this book, I encourage you to ask yourself, no matter what stage in life you are in, whether you are seeking the best life you can imagine.

While our journeys are different, we all have an opportunity to share our unique gifts with others. Each of us has the choice and the chance to enrich the lives of others.

On some of the coldest nights and during some of my saddest moments, memories of these encounters have renewed my spirit.

These stories remind me of how deeply I have been touched by my fellow life travelers, many of them strangers. Each one of them lifted my spirit. One by one, each person emblazoned the tapestry that has guided and enriched my life.

Thank you for reading my stories, some but fleeting moments, and others that occurred over time. As you pursue the life you seek, may you enjoy abundant blessings and wonderful memories.

Acknowledgments

I want to thank my children, Dena (Garry), Willie, (Lisa), and my grandchildren, Paris, Mason, and Marissa. All of them, in different ways, encouraged me to share these stories. My heartfelt thanks for your support and belief in the pursuit of my dream.

I also want to thank my Covenant Sisters, Merlyn, Nancy, and Rosezella for their support. Thanks to my sister, Myrtle, and my friends Karen, Minnie and Queen, who listened to my desire to write these stories and offered needed encouragement.

A special thanks to Peter, who has helped to make my dream a reality: that marriage can work and that real love endures. I am grateful for his unending belief in me, his untiring support, and the many hours of editing he provided in order to make these stories possible.

ABOUT THE AUTHOR

Ms. Loan received her undergraduate degree from the University of Maryland University College, and her graduate degree from George Washington University.

She spent most of her professional life in the management and promotion of wellness programs. She helped to establish and monitor eighteen School-Based Health Clinics in the United States, championed the rights of Nursing Home residents in the District of Columbia, and established and provided support to counseling programs for girls and women in the greater Washington DC metropolitan area. For twenty-five years Ms. Loan developed and led diversity training workshops for teachers, school administrators, healthcare and mental healthcare professions and others around the U.S.

Ms. Loan has traveled extensively and treasures the blessing of having met so many wonderfully diverse and interesting people during her life's journey.

Made in the USA
Middletown, DE
07 November 2020